Almost

by Nat Gabriel

illustrations by Elizabeth Wolf

Scott Foresman

Editorial Offices: Glenview, Illinois • New York, New York
Sales Offices: Reading, Massachusetts • Duluth, Georgia
Glenview, Illinois • Carrollton, Texas • Menlo Park, California

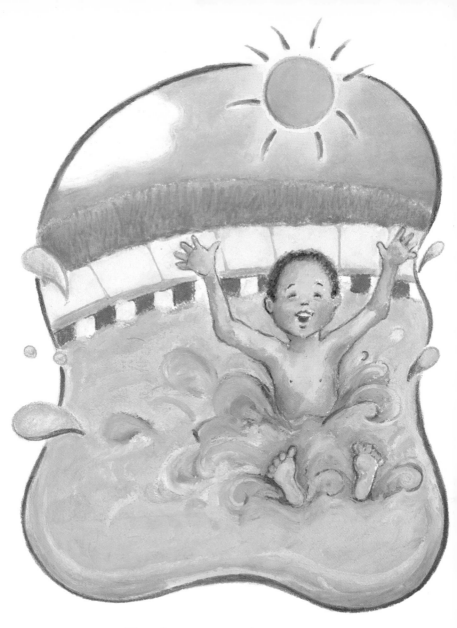

Ted jumped in.
He got wet all over.

Ned took a look.
He almost jumped in.
Almost, but not quite!

Ted jumped off.
He made a big splash.

Ned took a look.
He almost jumped off.
Almost, but not quite!

Ted jumped over.
He was having fun!

Ned took a look.
He almost jumped over.
Almost, but not quite!

Ted ran fast.

He jumped on a swing.

Ned took a look.
He almost got on.
Almost, but not quite!

Ted got an apple.
He almost took a big bite.
It looked yummy!

Ned did not get an apple.
He almost cried.
Almost, but not quite!

Ted gave Ned some of his apple.
"That is what friends are for,"
he said.

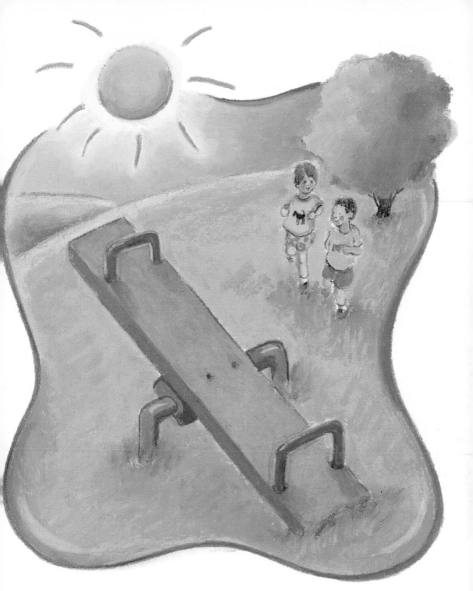

Ned and Ted ran fast.
Ned jumped on the seesaw.
"Get on!" he said.

13

Ted took a look.
He almost got on.
Almost, but not quite!

Ned had an idea.
"I can help," he said.

Ted got on the seesaw!
"Thanks for the help!" he said.
Ned smiled.
"That is what friends are for!"